W9-AIB-625

DOG OWNER'S GUIDE TO THE

German Shepherd

Dr. Malcolm Willis

FIREFLY BOOKS

A FIREFLY BOOK

Published by Firefly Books Ltd. 2005

Copyright © 2005 Ringpress Books Limited

First printing

Publisher Cataloging-in-Publication Data (U.S.)

Willis, Malcolm.

   German shepherd/Malcolm Willis.

[80] p. : col. photos. ; cm.
(Dog owner's guide)

Summary: A dog owner's guide to the care and training of German shepherds.

ISBN 1-55407-083-X

1. German shepherd dog. I. Title.
II. Series.

636.7376 22 SF429.G37W55 2005

Library and Archives Canada Cataloguing in Publication

Willis, Malcolm Beverley

   German shepherd/Malcolm Willis.
(Dog owner's guide)

ISBN 1-55407-083-X

1. German shepherd dog. I. Title.
II. Series.

SF429.G37W54 2005 636.737'6
C2005-900981-0

Published in the United States by
Firefly Books (U.S.) Inc.
P.O. Box 1338, Ellicott Station
Buffalo, New York 14205

Published in Canada by
Firefly Books Ltd.
66 Leek Crescent
Richmond Hill, Ontario L4B 1H1

Printed in China

ACKNOWLEDGMENTS

This book has been read and checked by my wife, Helen, whose suggestions have improved the text; any defects that remain must be laid at my door.

CONTENTS

1 SIMPLY THE BEST

Most dog breeders like to imagine that their breed goes back to antiquity. In fact, as dog breeds go, the German Shepherd is relatively modern. Its origins go back to Germany and the last two decades of the 19th century.

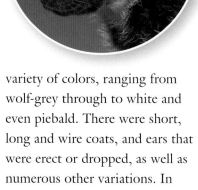

At that time, there existed in Germany a number of German sheepdogs which were of very mixed appearance. There were a variety of colors, ranging from wolf-grey through to white and even piebald. There were short, long and wire coats, and ears that were erect or dropped, as well as numerous other variations. In fact, these dogs were a mixture of types and a mixture of ancestry.

An unsuccessful attempt to set up a breed club was made in the late 1880s. Shortly afterwards, a

The German Shepherd was developed from a mixture of "sheepdog" types.

German cavalry officer called Max von Stephanitz established a society seeking to develop the mixed bag of German herding types into what, in German, was called the Deutsche Schäferhunde.

Von Stephanitz was a rather opinionated individual, but he was undoubtedly a leader. It was he who was the driving force behind the club (the Verein für Deutsche Schäferhunde or SV); he was behind the first Breed Standard, and he was the club's first president from its start in 1899 until his death in 1936.

CREATING THE GERMAN SHEPHERD

From mixed types available, it was decided to select a dog that had a short coat (rather than long or wire), that had erect ears and was of a dark color. Most early dogs were wolf-grey, but black-and-tan, and black were also acceptable. White dogs, such as the one pictured here, were not accepted. Initially, size was variable, and males ranged from under 24–27 inches (60–69 cm), while weight was light, at around 62–79 lbs (28–36 kg). The dog used as a prototype was Horand v Grafrath, registered as SZ 1. The letters SZ precede the number of any dog in the SV registration book or Zuchtbuch. The SV made rapid strides, holding its first Championship show in 1899.

DOG OF WAR

At the outbreak of World War I, the German Shepherd Dog (or Shepherd, as it became abbreviated), was the "war" dog of choice for the Kaiser's army. Prior to the 1914–1918 war, the Shepherd had not extended very far outside Germany, although examples had reached the United States and Britain, as well as other European countries. After the war, many army officers returned home with examples of the breed and, thereafter, its expansion was both dynamic and assured. Rin Tin Tin was actually a dog that an American soldier brought to the United States after World War I.

PUBLIC REACTION

The first German Shepherd registered with the American Kennel Club was in 1908, and the GSD Club of America was formed in 1913. The GSD Club of Canada (formed in 1922) is the oldest active breed club in the country. As in the U.K., the German Shepherd lost popularity in the United States and Canada during each of the world wars, but recovered quickly afterwards.

The Shepherd has a worldwide following.

In most countries, it would be true to say that the German Shepherd is among the most popular breeds where pedigree dogs are bred and exhibited. It is undoubtedly the most recognized breed of all.

In the United States, some 47,000 German Shepherds are registered every year and it was ranked the third most registered breed by the AKC in 2004.

Wolf Dog

Although the German Shepherd has been extremely popular throughout its history, it has also been much maligned. After the 1914–1918 war, it was much criticized as being a "wolf dog." In fact, the wolf is "in" every dog, since they all derived from a type of wolf.

In Australia, the breed was so severely criticized that, from the late 1920s through to the early 1970s, the importation of Shepherds was forbidden and, in most states, punitive taxes had to be paid, while breeding was often banned. The ban was imposed in the belief that the Shepherd

The wolf ancestry is evident in the German Shepherd.

would mate with the dingo and produce a formidable race of sheep killers.

Despite this level of prejudice, within a short time of the ban being lifted, the Shepherd was quickly the most popular breed in the country.

Loyal and intelligent, the Shepherd appeals to many different people.

THE VERSATILE SHEPHERD

The Shepherd is probably the most versatile of breeds. It may not be as good a tracker as the Bloodhound and, contrary to popular belief, it is not a particularly aggressive dog. It can, however, become very protective of its master's property; as, indeed, the Breed Standard requires. Nevertheless, in all-around merit, the Shepherd has no equal.

Throughout the world, it is the breed most often used by police, the armed services, or paramilitary groups. It has been one of the most

commonly used guide dogs for the blind; if it is now giving way on this count to Labradors and Golden Retrievers, it is partly because of the Shepherds' greater size, and also because Shepherds require more skilful and sensitive handling.

As a guard dog, the Shepherd's very reputation serves it well, and few dogs are as alert and watchful. Some owners have used the Shepherd to work the gun with considerable success, although its ear carriage is not suited to such work.

As an all-around dog, the German Shepherd is probably the best there is, and most of us who have been bitten by the Shepherd bug would argue that there is no breed that is as beautiful to behold at an extended trot, or that is as versatile. The breed is such that, once you have owned a Shepherd, there will be no other breed that will replace it in your affections.

HERDING INSTINCT

The original role of the German Shepherd was to work sheep and, in Germany and elsewhere, it is still to be found doing that job.

2 YOUR NEW PUPPY

The majority of breeders let their puppies go from 7 to 8 weeks of age and, in most cases, the puppy will be collected by the new owners.

If the pup has to undergo a long journey in countries such as the United States or Canada, it may have to be shipped by air instead.

GETTING READY

A few days before you are due to collect your puppy, check with the breeder to find out exactly what diet is being fed and make sure that you purchase the same type of food in advance. Remember that the puppy has to face the trauma of leaving the only home he has known, being separated from his siblings and his mother, plus making a journey either alone by air, or in a car. This is enough to upset any puppy, and the last thing he wants on top of this is a change of diet.

THE JOURNEY HOME

If you are going by car to collect your puppy, it is better to take someone with you to either hold the pup or, better still, take a traveling crate. The puppy can then be put in the crate and placed on the back seat alongside your friend or yourself, depending on who is driving. If you cannot recruit a friend and you are collecting the puppy on your own, the traveling crate is almost essential. I have known puppies travel on their first journey next to the driver, but it is potentially dangerous, especially if the puppy is lively.

If the journey is relatively short (an hour or so) then the puppy can probably make the journey without a stop. If the journey is lengthy, then a stop to give the puppy water may be necessary. The pup may want to relieve himself, but do not let him out of the car as he is not fully vaccinated. Let him relieve himself in the traveling crate, which you should have lined with old newspapers. You can clean up

Your pup will be safe and secure if he travels home in a crate.

It is a bewildering experience for a pup to leave his littermates and arrive in a new home.

lifting him out of the box and in the car. Do not let the puppy jump. Unless the journey is really lengthy, do not feed him, as the pup could well be sick if he is unused to car travel. If the car makes him sick, ensure that he does drink water.

on arrival at home. If you must stop en route, pull into a service station rather than stopping on the roadside. Accidents can happen, and agile puppies escape very easily, so do not park near a road.

You should travel equipped with a bowl and a plastic bottle or thermos full of fresh water. Your puppy can then have a drink, which he may well need to avoid some element of dehydration, depending upon the weather. Be gentle all the time: when you pick the puppy up,

Allow the pup to explore his surroundings.

ARRIVING HOME

When you get your puppy home, you can offer some food, but he may be disinterested. Although he is now home and safe on your premises, do not start getting him involved in lots of play. The puppy will be tired and stressed, even if he is of excellent character, so let him rest or, if he chooses, trot around after you as you do your household chores. Do not overtire your puppy.

CRATE-TRAINING

Collapsible steel-mesh crates are available in varying sizes, and from a variety of manufacturers. They form a standard part of pet equipment in the United States and Canada, and an increasing number of owners find them extremely useful.

From the start, accustom your dog to go into his crate and stay there, but do not use the crate for punishment. It may help if you feed your pup in his crate, so that he gets used to going in, and builds up a pleasurable association with his crate.

Puppies need a lot of rest, and most will appreciate having a place where they can sleep undisturbed. Children and

The puppy will soon view the crate as his own cosy den.

puppies get on well together, but children can play too long for most puppies. It is, therefore, invaluable to have a place where the puppy can be left in peace.

Even if you are at home all day, you will have occasion to go out at times and the pup has to be left behind. Young pups can get into mischief: all sorts of chewing on expensive furniture or endangering themselves by chewing on electrical cords, telephone wires, etc.

The advantage of using a crate is that you can go out knowing that the pup is safe from mischief and from harm. We use crates in this way, and young pups sleep in a crate at night. When they are

A pup needs to learn to settle on his own.

grown up, we find that our dogs will go into an open crate of their own volition, to find some peace and quiet. If they regarded the crate as a punishment, they would avoid it like the plague.

The crate must be big enough to accommodate a growing dog.

VITAL STATISTICS

The correct crate size to house an adult Shepherd is 49 x 27 x 30 inches (114 x 69 x 76 cm). This may look big to begin with, but you can make it cosy by placing a cardboard box or a small plastic bed lined with bedding, within the crate.

THE FIRST NIGHT

The first night may be a noisy one. The puppy may well cry, and you will be tempted to go down to see to him. Resist the temptation, unless you think the pup has some problem. The type of noise should tell you whether

anything is actually wrong.

If you suspect a problem, observe the puppy from a distance, preferably unobserved. If all is well, leave the puppy alone. If the pup is crated, he has less chance of getting into trouble than if he is just in a dog bed. If you go to your puppy and there is no problem he will quiet down but start up again as soon as you leave him.

Your first night, even the first few nights, may be disturbed by a crying puppy, but leave him alone or you will set a precedent that will be even harder to correct.

Try to harden your heart to your puppy's cries.

THE QUICK WAY TO

This training will start from the moment you take puppy home. With skill, it can be done inside seven days.

Your puppy will want to relieve himself after feeding, on waking, and during play. You must, therefore, be prepared to take the pup outside at such times, and you must go out with him.

Do not simply push the puppy into the yard and leave him there, or he will regard this as punishment.

Relief work

Go with your pup and encourage him. "Jack, hurry" will do, and when he relieves himself give him lots of praise. If you keep using the command "Jack, hurry," he will associate this with relieving himself and, as an adult, will usually respond to such a command.

Some breeders recommend laying down a newspaper, and putting the pup on it to relieve

HOUSEBREAK YOUR GERMAN SHEPHERD

Select a "toilet area" in the yard.

himself, using the command. Gradually, move the paper closer to the door as the puppy gets accustomed to using it, and then move the paper and pup outside until you eventually dispense with the newspaper. A clever pup will soon learn, and will go to the door when he wants to relieve himself. Make sure that you are there to let the puppy out, or you will undo the good work. To begin with, your pup will not be able to go through the night, so make sure he has some paper laid down that he can use for toileting. As he matures, he will be able to wait until he is let out in the morning.

Never chastise a pup when you find he has messed. A puppy will not associate

Always reward your pup when he performs outside.

19

the chastisement with the previously committed error, and things like rubbing your puppy's nose in the mess are simply useless. If you do catch your pup "in the act," say "No," firmly, scoop the pup up, rush him outside, and start the "Jack, hurry" routine, complete with praise.

TIMETABLE FOR HOUSEBREAKING

Take your puppy out at the following times, and he will soon learn to be clean in the house:

- first thing in the morning,
- after each meal,
- after a play session,
- every time he wakes up,
- if you see him sniffing and circling,
- last thing at night,
- every two hours (except at night), if he has not been taken out previously.

FEEDING

Feed your puppy as instructed by the breeder. This is the food the puppy is used to eating.

If you wish to change the diet, do so gradually, over a period of a few days.

The best way of doing this is to use a mixture of the old diet and the new diet, and then gradually reduce the original feed and increase the new one.

HEALTH CHECK

Within 48 hours of purchase, make sure that you take your puppy to your vet to have him checked over. If the puppy is ill, or if he has any serious defect, you should consider returning him. Take your vet's advice. The breeder should have supplied you with details of deworming treatments, and whether the vaccination program has been started. Your vet will tell you what vaccinations are necessary and when to return for them. While you are at the vet, do not put your puppy down; keep him on your lap, away from other dogs.

SETTLING IN

I am assuming that, having bought a puppy, at least one member of your household is at home during the day. No dog should be left alone for longer than four hours maximum, and this is best avoided with a young puppy.

When you are at home, make sure your pup gets lots of attention, but do not constantly

Spend time getting to know your new puppy.

fuss over him: you have bought a German Shepherd, not a toy.

Let your puppy follow you and be around you, and tickle his ears or his belly, but try to stop him jumping up and do not let him sit on the furniture. Play with your puppy by all means, going down on the floor with him and trying retrieving and other active games, but do not tire him out. A puppy will still play long after he has really had enough; use your judgement on this count.

Above all, get your puppy used to his name and to coming to you when called but, like all training, do not do things to excess.

TEETHING TROUBLES

In the next few weeks, your puppy will be teething and his mouth will be sore. Do not constantly maul your puppy's mouth to check his teeth. Remember, too, during teething, ear carriage is often erratic.

ROUTINE CARE

Groom regularly, using a soft brush and check the ears on a weekly basis. Do not pour anything into the ears as you can do more harm by messing about with them than by leaving them alone. The erect ear carriage of the Shepherd tends to bring fewer problems than soft ears, but it does not eliminate them.

Deworm your puppy once he is settled into your home, using a product recommended by your vet. Thereafter, deworm your Shepherd at regular intervals. Preventive measures against heartworm is required in parts of the United States and Canada.

Follow your vet's advice with regard to vaccinations, making sure you do not allow your pup to meet other dogs, or to go to places frequented by other dogs, until he is fully protected. Your vet will also advise you about booster shots.

Regular grooming from a young age will get your pup used to allover handling.

3 CARING FOR YOUR SHEPHERD

Now you have taken on a Shepherd, you are responsible for his needs for the duration of his life.

We are lucky that the Shepherd is a hardy breed and, if you pay attention to diet, grooming and exercise, your dog should thrive.

CHOOSING THE RIGHT DIET

Feeding is vital, not only to the health and wellbeing of your Shepherd, but to the influence it will have upon the dog's physical appearance. Although construction is largely predetermined by the genetic makeup of the dog, it is affected, to some degree, by the way the dog has been fed and reared.

In an extreme case, inadequate feeding could lead to rickets, which would affect leg length and construction to such a degree that the dog might bear little resemblance to its genetic potential.

Feeding begins before the dog is even conceived, since conception will be influenced by the nutritional status of the bitch at the time of mating. Animals that are well nourished are more likely to become pregnant than those that are not, or those in poor general condition.

During pregnancy, good nutrition is essential for the healthy development of the fetuses and, after birth, nutrition will influence the growth and health of the puppies.

Care with feeding is essential until the dog is an adult. Once fully grown, a dog may be fed less expensive foods on a maintenance basis, but this will depend upon the activities involved; an active stud dog, or a working animal, will require more than a maintenance diet.

There are three basic ways to feed dogs:

● Traditional: raw or cooked meat (often tripe) plus kibble.

● Canned food: this may be fed with or without kibble, depending on the type used.

● Complete diet: a dry food, although it can sometimes be fed in a moistened state. Often, this is nutritionally balanced to meet the differing needs of a dog depending on age and lifestyle. It is important to consider the pros and cons of each type of diet before deciding which to choose.

Good nutrition is essential for optimum results.

25

DRY FEEDS

The advantages of dry feeds are that they do not require refrigeration, and they are balanced diets (if from a reputable company) and, therefore, you do not need to add anything to them. They are easy to use, and can be served either dry or moistened, according to the manufacturer's instructions.

Usually, such diets are sold in varying amounts, from small bags to 44 lb (20 kg) paper sacks. It is better to buy unopened sacks rather than to buy in small quantities. Not only is it cheaper to buy in bulk but, when buying a small quantity from a store, it may be measured out from a bag

You do not need to add supplements to a complete diet.

that has been open for some time and may not be fresh. Stored badly or for too long, dry foods can become moldy and should then be discarded.

WHY CANNED FOODS CAN BE

These are easy to store (in a dry room) and to feed, but it is important to look at quality since some are quite poor (little better than offal), while others are highly digestible.

The price of canned food is often related to palatability and digestibility, with more palatable diets being more costly, as you would imagine. However, it is important to realize that many

TRADITIONAL

Unprocessed tripe is not high-quality meat, but it is cheap. Dogs tend to like it, and it usually firms up stools. It is much cheaper than dry or canned food, but it needs to be stored frozen, which is an added expense. Some breeders are staunch advocates of tripe and kibble, but such diets do need to be balanced with minerals and vitamins, and therein lies the difficulty. If you start adding calcium and vitamins, you can get it wrong and cause more harm than good.

There are a variety of other meats available. Like tripe, they need to be fresh and to be stored frozen. Failure to freeze fresh meat quickly can lead to it being contaminated by flies and other insects, especially in hot weather. Similarly, when thawing for use, such meats must be thoroughly defrosted and used quickly. They should not be fed in a semifrozen state.

THE ANSWER

of the brands on sale, and seemingly in competition with each other, are produced by the same manufacturer, so that competition is more imagined than real.

IMPORTANCE OF WATER

Water is essential to life. You can last longer without food than without water. Meat is made up of some 75 percent water and, though you may not think of your dog as meat, that is largely what his body is composed of. Water is an essential component of muscle, and it is needed for the excretory system. The kidneys are involved in this, and they require liquid intake to function effectively.

If a dog loses too much water from his tissues (about 10 percent), he could well die. In hot conditions, a dog will drink more than usual, as a means of trying to reduce body temperature. Similarly, appetite is affected by water, since the utilization of food requires the use of large amounts of water.

Some diets, such as canned food, are basically high in moisture content and will, therefore, lead to less water intake. Dry foods, however, need to accompanied by water. A hyperactive dog will probably have a high water requirement.

Fresh drinking water should always be made available.

DIETS TO FOLLOW ...

There are so many ways of feeding dogs, all with their own merits. However, in order to avoid giving innumerable menus, I will detail the diets used in our kennels. These have been used with both Shepherds and the larger, heavier-boned, Bernese Mountain Dogs. All have been successful diets and should be followed as stated.

... AND DIETS TO STICK TO

Some single-dog owners treat their dogs as fellow humans. Because humans do not eat the same food each day, they believe that dogs require the same constant change in their diets. Nothing could be further from the truth.

The dog needs the flora of his gut to be fairly static, and constant diet changes can alter this equilibrium. Keep to a proven diet that seems to suit your dog, do not chop and change.

Regular switches of diet are likely to upset your dog's digestive system, and you may well end up with a "faddy" eater for your pains.

THE THREE-STAGE GUIDE TO FEEDING

1. From 8 Weeks

At this age, the pup will travel to his new home. Having left his littermates, traveled in a car and found new surroundings and people, the puppy will probably be a bit upset and may not want to eat initially. Offer your pup the same diet as he was given by the breeder and do not introduce any changes.

Dogs may not eat for the odd day, but no dog will starve himself for too long, so do not be in a hurry to change to some other feeding regime. You, not the dog, should dictate diet.

Your puppy should be on four meals a day (available at all times), using such quantities as maintain growth without increasing bulk beyond the limited puppy fat seen in dogs of this age.

2. 6 Months

By 6 months, your dog should be reduced gradually to two meals per day. If you are feeding dry feed, this should never be reduced below two meals a day. Ideally, these should be fed in the morning, an hour or so after

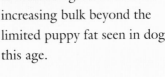

Your puppy should be on four meals a day when he first arrives in his new home.

YOUR PUPPY

exercise, and in the early evening, again one to two hours after exercise. Never feed just before exercise. With dry feeds, digestion is better with two meals a day, and bloat risks are reduced. If you feed tripe and kibble, feed them separately, as they digest better that way.

3. From 9 to 12 Months

At this age, you can start to change from a complete puppy diet to the next product. I would suggest a complete adult diet, designed for the average working dog.

Dogs should be fed these diets at the rate of about 2–3 oz per 10 lb (60–90 g per 4.5 kg). This is, of course, a daily amount, so it is fed in two halves.

I dislike having to weigh out food daily, nor is it necessary. If you know what the amount looks like when placed in a bowl, then it is easy enough to stick to that amount.

Your dog is growing in stature

You should be feeding to maintain steady growth as your dog matures.

until some 9 months of age, and gaining weight for even longer. He should be fed to maintain a steady growth, avoiding fattening, a bloated belly, and barrel ribbing. Your Shepherd should look lean and fit, never obese. Heart problems are often caused by overfeeding.

ADULT FEEDING

We feed at about 8 a.m. and between 4 p.m. 5 p.m., but this is not a rigid timetable. If dogs are fed strictly by the clock, they will learn to expect feeding and may start barking as the time approaches. Not being strict on time can be helpful on that count.

A dog in healthy condition and weighing about 79 lb (36 kg) should, if active and being fed a complete adult diet, be eating 20–30 oz (450–680 g) per day, or 10–15 oz (225–340 g) per meal.

Stick to a routine with mealtimes, but do not get tied into a rigid timetable.

Individual dogs vary in their metabolic rates. A dog who burns up calories quickly will stay lean on the top level, while another may be putting on weight.

You must, therefore, adjust diets up or down to maintain the right weight you require, or you must increase or decrease exercise.

Feeding is not just done by the book, but also on what your eye tells you about condition and weight.

SPECIAL NEEDS

Some manufacturers produce diets for the dog suffering from particular health problems. These are available through veterinarians and some pet stores. Such products can be valuable, but you must be sure that your dog really requires them.

OLD DOG ... NEW TRICKS!

As a dog ages, his metabolism will slow down and he will exercise less, and will thus need to eat less. Some manufacturers produce a special diet for veteran dogs. However, this aging process varies from dog to dog; it is not a fixed thing happening at a fixed age.

If your dog does show signs of age, then, as his level of exercise reduces, feeding should also be reduced, since being old does not necessitate being fat.

Some old dogs do have clinical signs of obesity, such as kidney or heart problems.

These dogs need veterinary help and may require a specialized diet.

GROOMING YOUR PUPPY

It is important to accustom your puppy to being groomed from an early age so he will learn to accept the attention.

Start off by brushing the coat with a soft brush so that the pup gets used to the sensation of being groomed. Pick up each paw in turn, and run your hand along his back to the tip of his tail, so that he gets accustomed to being handled. Feel along his tummy, and lift his tail to check the genital area. It is important that your pup understands that there is no such thing as a "no go" area. You should also examine the ears, eyes and mouth.

ADULT CARE

The Shepherd coat is relatively easy to care for, although it does shed profusely when the dog is molting. The best plan is to groom on a daily basis in order to keep the coat in good order. It also provides the opportunity to give your dog a general check over.

When the coat is shedding, a slicker brush will help to remove the hair. At other times, a bristle brush will be sufficient. If you want to bring out the shine in the coat, you can give a rubdown with a velvet cloth.

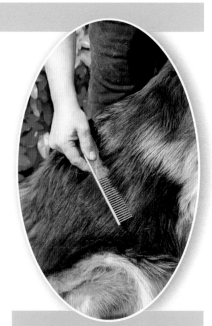

Groom every day to keep the coat in good order.

Long Coats

The long-coated Shepherd will need more attention, as the coat can mat and tangle. You will find a slicker brush is best for general care, and you will need a comb to tease out any mats that form. In most cases, the worst mats are found behind the ears, so remember to check this area.

It is also important to check your Shepherd's paws on a regular basis, as long hair can grow between the toes and between the pads. If this hair grows too long, it should be trimmed so that the dog is comfortable.

Ears

The erect ear carriage of a Shepherd is beneficial as it means the air can circulate freely, unlike in the drop-eared breeds, such as Spaniels. However, you should

UNWELCOME GUESTS

Fleas are always keen to find a home in a dog's coat, and you must be vigilant for any signs of telltale flea dirt in the coat. In fact, your Shepherd will soon let you know if he has fleas as he will be constantly scratching. However, if you treat your Shepherd regularly with a spot-on preparation, you will avoid the problem. Dogs can also pick up ticks, especially if you visit areas frequented by deer; Lyme disease (spread by deer ticks) is a serious disease in both dogs and humans, and preventive measures should be taken.

still check the ears to ensure they are clean and smell fresh. If you see signs of inflammation, excessive dirt or foul odor, consult your vet.

Nails

Unless your Shepherd has a lot of exercise on hard surfaces, his nails will need to be trimmed. You can use nail clippers to remove the tip of the nail, making sure you do not cut into the quick, which will bleed profusely.

If you are worried about trimming nails, ask your vet to show you what to do.

TOOTH CARE

Teeth will need to be cleaned regularly to prevent the buildup of tartar. You can use a fingerbrush or a long-handled toothbrush, and doggy toothpaste, which comes in a variety of meaty flavors. Most dogs soon learn to accept this procedure.

EXERCISE

Diet and exercise are closely related, since the diet you feed is largely dependent on your dog's energy requirements.

Dogs vary in the degree of exercise they need or want. Young pups are best exercising in their run, the house or the yard at their own pace. The occasional controlled exercise on a leash is undertaken more to socialize than as an exercise, as are visits to the training club.

By 6 months, controlled leash exercise can be undertaken, and this might amount to a couple of half-mile walks daily. As the dog matures he will need, and cope with, more exercise. A show dog who is exhibited, and hence needs to be in fit condition,

The Shepherd is an energetic dog who thrives on exercise.

Playing in the yard is all the exercise a young pup needs.

might have running exercise several nights a week, a couple of miles at a time.

Overexercise does more harm than good, and the excessive exercise of puppies can be detrimental to their health (i.e., contributing to conditions such as hip dysplasia). Dogs must be kept in a fit state: an adult male should weigh approximately 79 lb (36 kg) and an adult female 66 lb (30 kg). Your Shepherd should be weighed at regular intervals.

If a dog is too fat, he needs more exercise or less food, or both. If a dog is too thin, he needs more food, a worm check

or less exercise, if what he's getting seems to be excessive. Stud dogs, working dogs, and show dogs getting lots of activity, need to be fed well and exercised accordingly. However, youngsters under 12 months need cautious exercise, and should not be run for miles and miles.

Introduce some short sessions of controlled leash-walking.

4 TRAINING YOUR SHEPHERD

If you have a dog, there is a need to train that dog. If you have a bright, intelligent, large breed, such as the German Shepherd, then the need to train that dog becomes even more obvious.

A trained dog is a joy, an untrained and unruly dog can be a serious liability and, at a time when there is increasing pressure being placed upon dog owners, unruly dogs are the last thing anyone wants.

Although you need to train your Shepherd at home, both you and your dog will benefit from attending training classes. Nowadays, puppy playgroups are becoming increasingly popular and, if well organized, they can be very useful (provided your pup has been fully vaccinated).

When you progress beyond the playgroup, make sure you find a club with instructors who are used to training Shepherds.

In the following pages, the intention is to outline those elementary aspects of training, considered to be the basics of instruction.

THE BASIC PRINCIPLES

- Be consistent in the commands used. If you say "Down" to make the dog lie flat, then always say that. Do not alternate with "Get Down," "Lie Down," "Flat," etc.

- Use short commands that cannot be confused with others. However much you may talk to your dog at other times, when training, be economical with words. Remember also that the tone is important and should reflect the instruction or praise being given.

- Call your dog by a name and keep to it. Your Shepherd may have a registered name that is several syllables long, but he will probably be called by a short name of one or two syllables. Always use that name. If your bitch is called "Annie," then always use that in training—not "Ann" or "Old Girl" or "Lass" or any of the multiplicity of names you will find a dog called by different members of the family.

- Make training enjoyable. Do not overdo it to the extent that the dog becomes bored. Do not try to do too much too soon.

- Do a little bit each day, however brief.

- Remember that you can teach an old dog new tricks, but it is easier with an old dog who was taught other tricks in his youth.

Make training sessions fun for you and your dog.

PHASES OF LEARNING

In training a dog, we are seeking to modify behavior, and it is, therefore, necessary to examine the behavioral periods of the dog. Research in the United States over a long period of time established that dogs have specific periods in early life during which learning is, or is not, advanced.

Neonatal

This lasts from birth to about 14 days of age. During most or all of this time, the pup is blind and deaf. His behavior is largely confined to suckling his mother. During this period, it is useful to handle each pup on a daily basis but, during these first two weeks, the pup is relatively well insulated against psychological damage and learns little.

Transitional

This lasts from approximately 14 to 21 days. During this week, the pup is moving from neonatal life towards a more adult system. The eyes will open around day 13, and the ears function soon afterwards. The pup can now see, hear and walk, instead of crawl. Teeth are erupting, and semisolid food can be eaten. The pup is now conditionable in the sense that he can develop the capacity for learning.

Socialization

This period runs from 3 to 12 weeks of age. During this time, the dog will develop attachments towards others dogs and

A puppy should learn how to interact with other dogs and humans during his socialization period.

humans, even if contact with humans is fairly limited to the immediate family of the breeder.

During this period, the pup is weaned from his mother and, in the period around 7 to 8 weeks, he will probably be sold to his new owner.

In this period, socialization is crucial. Pups should never leave the nest (in the sense of being sold) prior to 4 weeks of age and, ideally, not before 7 to 8 weeks.

However, they must be in their new home before 12 weeks of age, or be settled in the breeder's home if being retained.

Juvenile

This period runs from 12 weeks to sexual maturity, which may be as early as 5 months, but is usually closer to 9 months.

By now, the puppy is in his new home but, in the early part of the period, he is not fully vaccinated.

DON'T WAIT!

Failure to socialize a pup by 12 weeks of age can have a marked and adverse effect upon subsequent character development.

The German Shepherd

The puppy, therefore, needs to be socialized, but not exposed to the risks of contracting disease. Most experienced breeders compromise by taking a partially vaccinated dog out of the home environment to socialize him, while taking care to avoid contact with strange dogs. Dogs that are restricted to kennel life after 12 weeks will be severely handicapped in many cases.

Often, the "pick of the litter," retained by the breeder, will develop less well in character than his siblings, who have lived in homes and in a family environment, while the pick of the litter languishes in a kennel. During the juvenile period, a dog must be exposed to all kinds of experience: other dogs, other animals, different humans, noise, traffic, car rides, etc. A comprehensive program of socialization during this period will result in great benefits in terms of the correct development of the dog's character.

Some dogs are inherently weak in character because their pedigrees are full of nervous ancestors; such dogs are unlikely to develop the correct

The juvenile pup needs to encounter new experiences.

BEWARE OF FEAR

Few owners will want a cowardly dog and, to this end, never buy a puppy if he cowers in the nest, or if his mother is fearful. A fearful dog is unreliable and essentially untrustworthy with strangers, although he may be perfectly good in his home with the family.

temperament, however well they may be socialized. There is ample evidence that inherently sound temperaments can be damaged by inadequate or incorrect socialization.

Dogs vary in character and, hence, in the way they adjust to the family. Some dogs are pack leaders and, as they get older, they will express this leadership in little clashes with authority—yours. By 24 months of age, such a dog may be difficult to control, unless you have taken him in hand earlier. Properly controlled, these pack-leader dogs are possibly the best dogs to own, but they are not suitable for inexperienced, first-time owners, or those owners who are not sufficiently masterful.

Most pet owners want what might be termed an "easygoing" dog, who will be sound in temperament, but not an innate leader.

All dogs vary in character and the pup's personality will be clear from an early age.

TRAINING EXERCISES

The main exercises for basic obedience are: Sit, Down, Stay, Come and Heelwork. They should be tried in short bursts each day, making sure that your dog is never bored with them.

Asking the dog to sit before he is fed reinforces his training.

Teaching the Sit

This is one of the first, and easiest, exercises to learn. You can start soon after your puppy has come to live with you.

When training dogs, the custom is to walk the dog on your left. With your puppy, stand him on your left and, simultaneously, say "Sit" and press down gently on the dog's rump. When the puppy sits, give plenty of praise and keep the dog in the Sit for a moment.

If you do this regularly, your dog will soon learn the command and will sit regardless of where he is in relation to you.

You can do it with the dog on a leash, in which case, as you say "Sit," you pull up slightly with the leash. Many owners train their dogs to sit before being fed, and this is usually successful. However, it gets the dog accustomed to believe in a reward (food) for sitting, when, in reality, he will need to do it without reward (other than praise).

TEACHING YOUR SHEPHERD TO COME WHEN CALLED

Getting your dog to come to you on command is the most important exercise he has to learn. From the very start, you must give your dog a name and use it. For example, if you call your dog "Jack," regularly use that name and no other. He will soon learn it and, when he comes to you on hearing it, praise or reward him (although I am not personally a fan of food rewards). Your dog will soon respond and, once he knows his name, you can start to recall him with a command such as "Jack, Come."

You must insist that he responds, and praise him when he does. If he will not come, repeat the instruction and either sit down or move away from him and, in either case, he will be curious enough to follow or approach. Praise him.

Work at building up an enthusiastic response to the recall.

Once your dog is out in a field, he still needs to be instructed. If you have difficulties, an extending leash may be used and, on the command "Jack, Come," he can be gently reeled in. Always, if you command him to come, make sure that he does. Do not give up on him, and always praise him when he arrives.

THE CHASE ISN'T ON

Never chase after your puppy, or he will learn that as a game.
If he will not learn to come, repeat the exercise with a leash and, as you
say "Jack, Come," give him a tug to bring him towards you.

WALKING TO HEEL

You can start this at around
4 months of age, although
you can accustom your pup to
wearing a collar prior to this.

The aim is for the dog to walk
on your left, with his head just
ahead of your knee. Start from
the sit position, then give the
command "Jack, Heel," and start
to move, leading off with your
left foot.

Give a short jerk on the leash
as you move, and the dog will go
with you.

Actually, first time, the pup will
probably go ahead of you, as far
as the leash will allow. You should
hold the leash in your right hand
and, as the dog bounds forward,

Keep leash-training sessions short and fun,
or your Shepherd will become bored.

turn to your right and go back to where you were. Command the dog "Jack, Heel," and give him a tug to turn him around.

Walk up and down for a short time, trying to keep your puppy alert and walking more or less to heel. Then command "Sit," and stop the exercise. If you repeat this on a daily basis, the dog will eventually catch on and learn to walk on your left.

It is sound policy to make heelwork sessions fairly short, finish with the dog sitting, and then have a play after each session.

TEACHING THE DOWN

Start from the Sit, with the dog on the leash on your left. Give the command "Down," and, as you do so, apply gentle pressure to the dog's shoulders, so he is encouraged to go into the correct position.

Bend down with your dog to maintain the Down position, then release him, giving plenty of praise.

Repeat this a few times, gradually extending the time the pup stays in position.

You can then start to give the command when you are standing upright, practice a few times and your puppy will soon get the idea.

It is useful to have a release command, such as "OK," which you can use when the exercise is finished. Your pup will learn that it is the signal for him to break position.

SECRETS OF THE STAY

This can be divided into two sections: the Sit-stay and the Down-stay, depending on whether you want the dog to stay seated or lie flat.

The principle is the same, but it may be slightly easier to teach from the Down position.

- Position your dog on the left and command "Sit" or "Down," and then hold your left palm in front of the dog's face and command "Stay." Now, step ahead of the dog by a few yards.

- Repeat the command more than once. Turn and face the dog, still holding your palm as a deterrent. Return to the dog's right-hand side and praise him—still in the Sit-stay or Down-stay—before allowing the dog to get up and move.

The first time will not be that easy. The likelihood is that the dog will follow you. In which case, put the dog straight back into position and repeat the exercise.

Repeat daily, moving only a few yards away, until the dog seems to be staying as left. Then, and only then, go further away.

Once the dog remains in position while you move well away, try the exercise out of sight. However, make sure you use a location where you can move out of the dog's sight but can keep

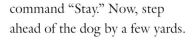

The Sit-stay: A confident hand signal encourages the dog to stay put.

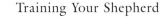

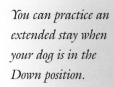

You can practice an extended stay when your dog is in the Down position.

the dog in your view. The Down-stay or Sit-stay when out of sight is something that will come later rather than sooner but, by then, the dog should be reliable at the Stay. At the finish of a Stay, release the dog with a "Good boy," or a similar release command, so that he knows the exercise is over.

THE RETRIEVE

Most pups will chase after a thrown object and, long before you start retrieve training, you should be indulging in play that encourages your pup's retrieving instinct. Play by throwing articles that the dog knows and will, therefore, chase and usually mouth or pick up. When he does pick up an item, encourage him to "Come," thus starting the retrieve habit. We try this with everything from car keys to blocks of wood. You can modify this by retrieving hidden articles: initially letting the dog see where you hide them and, as the dog becomes adept at finding them, hide them without his seeing. A command such as "Jack, Fetch" will stimulate the dog, and most pups enjoy the game.

HIDE-AND-SEEK

Playing hide-and-seek encourages the dog to use his nose and instills a retrieve instinct. When the time comes to try in earnest, first teach your dog to hold the retrieve object, e.g. the dumbbell, by putting it in the dog's mouth, and giving the command "Hold." Make sure the dog continues to hold the object, but in such a way as not to hurt his mouth. Once your dog will hold the object, it is easy enough to get him to pick it up and carry it. From then on, the command "Jack, Fetch" can be combined with "Hold" and "Jack, Come," and finally, "Sit," so that the dog chases, picks up, brings back, and sits holding the object.

MAKING PROGRESS

These few simple exercises are adequate for most dogs and owners. If you find you have a clever dog and you have some talent as a trainer, then you can go further into Competitive Obedience, or even Working Trials and Schutzhund.

Many Shepherds have good noses, and the hide-and-seek type of game can be extended to make a dog learn the rudiments of tracking. Throughout, work must be made enjoyable with lots of praise and play. You can use toys with a dog, but be careful in your choice. If you allow your pup to have an old shoe, don't complain when the dog demolishes your brand-new pair. Try to use objects meant for dogs, rather than those derived from old clothes, since this encourages a dog to play with all clothes, even new ones!

Always encourage your dog to play and to retrieve. If you are sitting together in the house, get your dog to chase objects and pick them up, but never let this go on too long.

SUMMING UP ...

The German Shepherd is a highly intelligent dog who thrives on mental stimulation. Do not neglect this aspect of caring for your dog, or he may well use his intelligence to become deviant. Make training part of your regular routine, and your relationship with your dog will be enriched by the time spent together.

5 THE "IDEAL" SHEPHERD

All pure dog breeds have been selected over the years to represent a specific ideal. This ideal is epitomized in what is called the Breed Standard, which is a description, in words, of what the breed is supposed to look like.

Breed Standards were usually drawn up by early enthusiasts of the breed, working as a group, and their descriptions have formed the basis of what the breed has been selected to resemble. Some Standards have been well written and intelligently drawn up, while others have been drawn up in a way that leaves many inaccuracies and deficiencies. The Standard of the German Shepherd was first drawn up by the SV in 1899, under a group led by von Stephanitz. The original version has been revised many times (1901, 1909, 1930, 1961 and 1976), and each country has tended to use a version of the SV Standard translated into the appropriate language.

A Standard is a kind of prototype of what the dog should look like, and it is up to breeders and judges to interpret that

Standard. However, not everyone interprets the words in the same way, and so differences of opinion can occur, leading to faulty judging and breeding.

I will list each heading of the Standard in turn, and comment accordingly.

CHARACTERISTICS OF THE GSD

The main characteristics of the German Shepherd Dog are steadiness of nerves, attentiveness, loyalty, calm self-assurance, alertness and tractability. These characteristics are necessary for a versatile working dog. Good temperament is essential, and shy and vicious dogs should be severely penalized in the ring and rejected from breeding programs. Judges ignoring such features are doing the breed a disservice, and their competence is in question.

STOP

MUZZLE

WITHERS

TOPLINE

CROUP

STIFLE

HOCK

CHEST

PASTERN

TUCK UP

GENERAL APPEARANCE

The immediate impression of the Shepherd is of a dog slightly long in comparison to his height, with a powerful and well-muscled body. The relation between height and length is so interrelated as to enable a far-reaching and enduring gait. The coat should be weatherproof.

A true-to-type Shepherd gives an impression of innate strength, intelligence and suppleness, with the mental attributes to make him always ready for tireless action as a working dog. Overall, he should present a harmonious picture of nobility, alertness and self-confidence.

Without training, it is difficult to imagine most dogs fitting the ideal described above, but the Standard emphasizes that the Shepherd should be a calm dog of excellent, trustworthy character. It suggests a dog that is readily handled, but not one that is leaping over everyone and making friends with every stranger he meets. It also suggests a dog that is a "defense" dog, not an attack dog.

The proportions of length (front of the chest to the rear of the pelvis) to height (to the wither) are such that the dog is longer than he is tall.

In the United States, the ideal proportions are 10:8.5 (AKC). In Canada they are 10:8 (GSDCC). Excessive body length is not desirable.

THE HEAD

The Shepherd is not a "head" breed in the sense that excessive emphasis is placed upon the head, almost as if it were the most important feature. Nevertheless, a correct head is of importance.

The German Shepherd Dog Standard simply calls for a head that fits the body. Thus, a very strong and large head would not be suitable in a small male, and a small head would be unacceptable in a big dog. Secondary sexual characteristics must be obvious, so that the sex of the animal is identifiable from the head.

The fact that the skull is defined as half the whole head-length suggests that long-muzzled animals are not desired. Similarly, "lippiness" is not desired; tight-fitting, "clean" lips are needed, free from looseness.

The underjaw should be visible when the mouth is closed, and some evidence of a stop should exist, but it must not be excessive. Long heads are often linked to faulty bites and missing teeth.

The Shepherd's sex should be identifiable from the head.
Female (left) and male (right).

THE EYES HAVE IT

The Standard is explicit in calling for a medium-sized and almond-shaped eye, so both a round eye or a large, protruding one are undesirable. A dark rather than a light-colored eye is preferable, but care must be taken to relate eye color to coat color. An eye that will look acceptable in a brown face might look lighter in a black face, and so color should not be penalized to excess. Claims that light eyes see better are without proof, and suggestions that light eyes are associated with greater intelligence are tenuous.

ALL ABOUT THE EARS

Ear size is relative to head size, but they should be medium rather than large or small. Tipped ears, as seen in Collies, and hanging (soft) ears are quite unacceptable, as they destroy the whole appearance of the dog.

In recent years, some dogs have ears that, while erect, are rather weak in muscle, and this is often obvious in movement. Although many judges like a dog to run with his ears erect, it is not a requirement as long as the ears are firm and can be erected as the dog requires.

It is important to realize that all Shepherds are born with hanging ears, and these become erect during early puppyhood. Ear carriage can be erratic during the teething period, as illustrated in the picture above.

MOUTH AND BITE

The jaws must be strongly developed and the teeth should be healthy, strong and complete in number. There should be 42 teeth, 20 in the upper jaw and 22 in the lower jaw.

The Shepherd has a scissor-bite; i.e., the incisors in the lower jaw are set behind the incisors of the upper jaw, and they meet in a scissor grip in which part of the surface of the upper teeth meet and engage part of the surface of the lower teeth.

Although the odd missing tooth would have minimal effect

upon a pet dog, specialist judges tend to take a hard line on missing teeth, and penalize the dogs.

In most Breed Surveys, a missing tooth prevents a dog from being given a Class 1 grading. As a result, unlike many other breeds, faulty dentition is relatively uncommon.

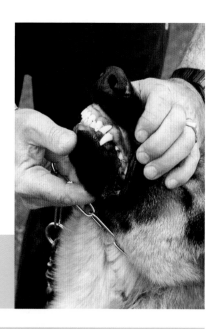

The Shepherd has a scissor-bite, with the top teeth closely overlapping the bottom ones.

NECK AND FOREQUARTERS

The neck is relatively long, but not excessively so, and it is carried forward rather than upwards. Long "swan" necks are undesirable, and dogs should not move with the head held erect because this will reduce their forward reach. Some dogs that have erect-held heads have forward-placed shoulders, which is clearly faulty construction.

Shoulder blades should be long, set obliquely (45 degrees), and laid flat to the body. The ideal shoulder angulation between the shoulder blade (scapula) and upper arm (humerus) is said to be 90 degrees but, in reality, a slightly larger angle might be more ideal. A very steep front assembly or a forward-faced scapula will restrict movement, but the most crucial feature is bone length.

As a trotting dog, the Shepherd needs a long scapula and a long humerus. A short upper arm will lead to the dog dropping on the forehand in motion, unless "lifted up" by the handler pulling on the leash.

Shoulder Placement

A correctly placed shoulder should allow a plumbline dropped mid-wither to lie just behind the back of the foreleg.

A well-developed chest should not be mistaken for a good front assembly; often, forward-placed shoulders are seen with well-developed forechests. Similarly, a steep, forward-placed front assembly may give the desired high wither, but this is not the correct way to achieve a high wither.

Legs should be straight, with the feet not turned out in an east–west pattern. The Shepherd should have an angled pastern; not a straight one as seen in most breeds. An excessive angle is a weakness.

A very deep chest is not required, but a Shepherd does need long forelegs. Short forelegs are not associated with good movement.

The Shepherd's long shoulder blades hark back to his days as a trotting, herding dog.

THE BODY

The length of the body should exceed the height at the wither: the correct proportions being given as 10:8.5 (U.S.) or 10:8 (Canada). In modern times, some dogs are too short in body, and that is not desired.

The chest is only 45 to 48 percent of the height and must not come below the elbow. Ribs should be oval, not barreled or flat, and should be long from front to back so that the loin is relatively short.

A long loin is a sign of weakness in movement. Some tuck-up at the loin is needed, but not excessively so, as in a sighthound (e.g., Greyhound).

The belly should be strong and firm, not flabby. This latter aspect requires the dog to be in fit condition, but some lines do produce flabby bellies.

The back should be relatively short, with length coming from the front and rear assemblies as well as the middle-piece. Long backs are associated with weakness, and will dip in movement more often than not. However, an arch (roach) in the center of the back is not wanted, nor should the croup start from the center of the back. The croup is over the pelvis, and should be long and gently curved.

The Shepherd's back should be relatively short, and a slight tuck-up should be noticeable.

HINDQUARTERS

The dog should have a broad thigh, with good length of leg bones to the hock. Angulations at the rear should match those at the front if the dog is to have a balanced gait. Any imbalance between front and rear angulations will lead to crabbing (running at an angle rather than straight), or to excessive pickup of the forefeet, or high backlift of the rear pastern.

PAWS AND MOVEMENT

Paws should be rounded, with well-arched toes. Pads should be well cushioned and durable, and nails should be short, strong and dark in color.

Most Shepherds are born without hind dewclaws, as this is a recessive trait and most Shepherds carry the gene in duplicate. If present, hind dewclaws must be removed, but front dewclaws are left alone.

Paws are not always good in the breed, tending to be longish and harelike, rather than round and compact. However, splayed feet are rare, although most dogs will splay their feet on soft ground. Shepherd movement, at its best, is a joy to behold. The flow of the legs, the firmness of the back, and the effortless way that a well-moving Shepherd trots, is a unique feature of the breed, which no other breed comes anywhere near.

Good movement is not, however, assessed in terms of speed but in terms of ground cover. The dog covering the most ground with the least effort is the most desirable in movement terms. Generally, a dog with correct conformation is likely to show the best movement.

Movement should be energy efficient, with the dog covering the most ground with as little effort as possible.

However, movement is also a mental thing. Some Shepherds just love to gait, while others, no less well constructed, are bored by the show ring and move without enthusiasm; yet, in the freedom of the field, this dog might move just as well as the outstanding show gaiter. Getting a dog enthusiastic about gaiting is thus important to his show career.

Side gait should be far reaching with good hind thrust, the power coming up through the back towards the wither, which will lower only slightly as the head is thrust forward rather than upwards. The back will be firm with minimal up-and-down motion. Dogs who paddle are usually not balanced in front or rear angulation, and the dog holds his front leg in the air that fraction longer to maintain the sequence of steps. From the front and rear, the dog will be sound.

Thus, the front feet will move in towards the center, but with the leg straight and relative to the foot. The faster the movement, the more the feet will be placed centrally.

The rear pasterns will be straight and more or less parallel, driving but not lifting too high when extended backwards. Rear pasterns should be relatively short, not long.

E IS THE KEY!

The Shepherd gait is epitomized by the two "E"s of Endurance and Economy. A good Shepherd should move without effort and be capable of prolonged movement. To do this, he must be a physically fit dog, and thus, gaiting is not only about construction and mental willingness: it also requires a dog that is trained, and in athletic, fit condition.

THE COAT

The Shepherd should have a double coat, consisting of a thick undercoat, and a hard, flat outercoat, which should be as dense as possible. Long coats are popular among pet owners, but are biologically less acceptable because the coat is less weather resistant and they are, therefore, unlikely to be successful in the show ring. About 10 percent of Shepherds are born with long coats, and about half the short-coated Shepherds carry the long coat allele recessively. A long coat can only be identified at around 6 to 8 weeks, i.e., about the time the puppy is sold.

Long coats are attractive, but do not strictly adhere to the Breed Standard.

TAIL PIECE

The tail should be bushy-haired and, at rest, should hang in a saberlike curve. Short tails, not reaching to the hock joint, are rare, as most reach the mid-pastern. Slight sideways bends are tolerated, but tails that lift high in movement, or that curl, are to be severely penalized.

QUESTION OF COLOR

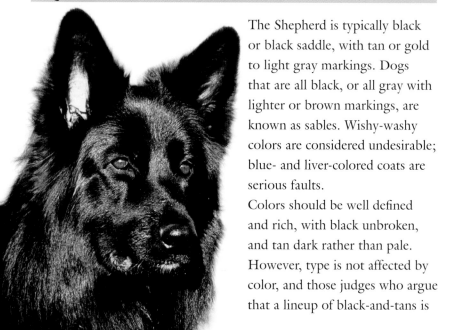

The Shepherd is typically black or black saddle, with tan or gold to light gray markings. Dogs that are all black, or all gray with lighter or brown markings, are known as sables. Wishy-washy colors are considered undesirable; blue- and liver-colored coats are serious faults.

Colors should be well defined and rich, with black unbroken, and tan dark rather than pale. However, type is not affected by color, and those judges who argue that a lineup of black-and-tans is

The black color is rare, but it is allowed in the Breed Standard.

marred by the insertion of a gray or black dog ought not to be judging. Color is not type. White dogs are disqualified from the show ring in the United States and Canada. This stems from the fact that white dogs are less acceptable as guards because they are visible; while as herders, a white dog is less useful. If you ever work a white sheepdog on snow-covered hills, you will see why.

White-coated dogs are disqualified from the show ring, but they are popular with pet owners.

HEIGHT

The ideal height, according to the American Standard (measured to the highest point of the wither), is 22–24 inches (56–60 cm) for females and 24–26 inches (60–66 cm) for males.

Increasingly, the breed has become somewhat larger, so that a 25-inch (64-cm) male would look small in most show rings around the world. There is a need to reduce size, but it must not be done by putting inferior 25-inch (64-cm) dogs over superior 26-inch (66-cm) animals.

Clearly, very large heights — 27 inches (69 cm) and above in males — must be penalized, however good they may be in construction; but it must be done gradually, if correct type is to be preserved.

Body weights will vary with stature. A male might range from 75–100 lb (34–45 kg), or even more, depending on his height. However, excessive weight will detract from the dog's endurance, and most Shepherd males would be in the 80 lb (36 kg) range; females would be several pounds lighter.

The male Shepherd is taller than the female.

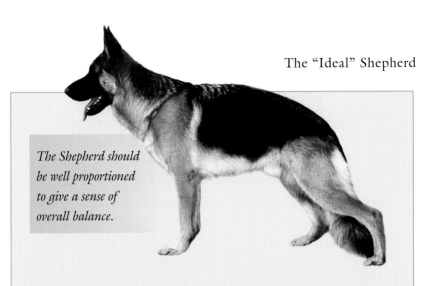

The Shepherd should be well proportioned to give a sense of overall balance.

UNDERSTANDING THE MEANING OF TYPE

Type is not about color, nor is it about size. A 26-inch (66-cm) dog and a 23.5-inch (60-cm) dog could be of different colors, of clearly different size, and yet could be identical in type.

Type is about proportions. The relationship of body length to height at wither, the length of muzzle relative to skull, chest depth to height, upper arm to scapula, and many other relationships and proportions are all features of type and must be understood.

The so-called British Alsatian of the 1980s and 1990s is of incorrect type because he has proportions that do not match those laid down in the Standard. He is, therefore, of a different type to the international kind of Shepherd seen throughout Europe, South Africa, Australasia and Britain.

A judge may prefer a smaller male, but the important factor is the proportion of length to height: 10:8.5 (United States) or 10:8 (Canada). Despite their size differences, does, in this aspect of proportion, of identical type. Whether they were overall of identical type would depend upon other proportions. Until you can understand proportions in the Shepherd, you cannot understand his type.

6

GENETIC CONDITIONS

I n all breeds and in all species, defects occur that are undesirable in that they are aesthetically unappealing, or they can or do lead to an impaired lifestyle on the part of the dog.

In some cases these defects are acquired problems, caused by disease or injury but, in other cases, the defect is inherited.

No self-respecting breeder wants to encourage inherited defects, though all breeders, however careful, will have their share of problems.

This chapter does not seek to be comprehensive in respect of inherited defects seen in the breed, but it lists, in alphabetical order, some of the more common inherited defects known to exist.

BLUE COAT COLOR

This is a simple recessive trait caused by the presence of the gene d in duplicate. Normal-colored dogs are DD, but some are Dd in genetic makeup. Such dd animals are born with a bluish sheen, making them look like sables, which they are not. Most blues (dd) lose their blue sheen with time and end up black-and-tans or sables.

Cancer

Numerous cancers occur in the dog, and it is believed that some of these may have a genetic basis and/or that some breeds are genetically predisposed towards them.

The Shepherd, as a breed, is not particularly at greater risk of cancer than the average for all breeds. Thus, although dogs may die of lymphosarcoma (lymph cancer) or osteo-sarcoma (bone cancer), among others, the Shepherd is not at high risk from these cancers.

Cataracts

In the early 1980s, juvenile cataract was seen in a few dogs. The cataract was present in early puppyhood, and was certainly obvious by 12 months of age.

The mode of inheritance is a simple autosomal recessive, but has a low incidence in the breed. Affected dogs should

Like most breeds, the Shepherd is prone to some health disorders.

not be bred from. (Cataracts in old dogs are part of the aging process, and are acquired rather than inherited). The condition still occurs at rare intervals.

Degenerative Myelopathy

This is a relatively common disease in the Shepherd, where it is more frequent than in any other breed. It is seen from middle age (5 years or so), but it can occur in younger animals.

The condition develops over a period of months, usually beginning with some hind limb lameness, but it is not to be confused with hip dysplasia, since it is the spinal cord that is degenerating. The dog retains bladder control but, increasingly, has difficulty with hind limbs, eventually becoming paraplegic.

Most dogs are euthanized as the disease progresses but, if left, there is further degeneration, loss of bladder control, and paralysis. The mode of inheritance, if any, is unknown.

The Shepherd generally has good dentition, but some faults can occur.

Cryptorchidism

Failure of the testicles to descend into the scrotum is termed cryptorchidism, and can be either unilateral (one descended) or bilateral (neither descended). Breeders often refer to unilateral cases as monorchids, but the true monorchid only possesses one testicle, whether descended or not. About 4 percent of Shepherd males will be cryptorchids, most of these unilateral. Bilateral cases are sterile.

Dental Faults

In modern times, the Shepherd has tended to have good dentition.

The most serious fault is an undershot jaw, which occurs when the lower incisors protrude in front of the upper. This is exceedingly rare in the Shepherd. A more common failing is an overshot bite, when the upper incisors are ahead of, and touching, the lower.

CAUSES OF EPILEPSY

Epilepsy simply means "seizure," so that any dog who has seizures can be termed an epileptic. Essentially, the problem results from incorrect electrical stimuli in the brain. The cause of epilepsy can be varied: physical damage to the brain, cancer, certain kinds of poison, certain diseases, and even heavy parasitic loading or teething might give rise to seizures some instances. All of these causes, and others, are acquired, and the dog should not have a seizure again if these acquired features are corrected. However, there is a condition seen in the Shepherd (and other breeds) termed primary or idiopathic epilepsy. There is considerable evidence to suggest that this is an inherited condition.

HEMOPHILIA A

Hemophilia A is a blood disease wherein the blood does not clot quickly enough. The condition is seen in humans as well as many dog breeds. In the Shepherd, it is of a moderate, as opposed to a mild or severe, nature. The clotting of blood is controlled by several genetically controlled factors, and Hemophilia A is connected with Factor VIII. The condition is a sex-linked trait carried on the X chromosome, and there are five genetic kinds of Shepherd.

HERNIAS

A hernia is a protrusion of an organ from the abdominal cavity through an opening. Hernias can be inguinal (usually scrotal), perineal (anal), diaphragmatic (the diaphragm), and umbilical (the umbilicus).

Diaphragmatic hernias are almost always caused by injury, and inguinal hernias are so rare in the Shepherd as to be safely ignored. Although perineal hernias have been seen in the Shepherd, they are also rare.

Umbilical hernias, usually seen at or soon after birth, are known

Umbilical hernias affect only eight out of 1,000 Shepherd pups.

in the Shepherd, but at a low frequency of about eight cases per 1,000 births. It is inherited in a threshold fashion and caused by several genes. Severe cases should not be bred, but minor cases might be used if the animal is of outstanding merit.

THE FACTS ABOUT HIP DYSPLASIA

The hip joint is a ball-and-socket joint, in which the femoral head (ball) should fit tightly into the acetabulum (socket). First reported in 1935, HD is found in many breeds and exists when the hip joint is badly constructed. Usually, the cause is a shallow acetabulum but, at all events, dysplastic dogs can vary from minor flaws through to quite severely dislocated hip joints. In middle age, dysplastic dogs can become arthritic, which is a painful condition and a principal disadvantage of dysplasia. Although most research has been done with the Shepherd, the breed is by no means the worst affected. The condition is inherited, with a heritability of 40 percent in the

German Shepherd. This means that 40 percent of any superiority (or inferiority) in the parents (in respect of hips), will be transmitted to the offspring.

Although excessive exercise in youth, along with excess body weight, might play a part, HD is mainly caused by genetics and can only really be corrected by breeding.

LIVER COAT COLOR (BROWNS)

Most Shepherds are genetically BB and, therefore, can produce black pigment even if they are white dogs. Dogs carrying the B genes will always have a black nose.

Some dogs are Bb and, though they appear perfectly normal, two such Bb animals could give rise to a number of bb offspring. Such dogs cannot form black pigment and are liver-colored, where they would otherwise have been black. This includes the nose leather.

In addition, the bb combination causes lighter eye color. Although biologically not disadvantaged, the bb dog is not normally exhibited. The bb combination does not affect non-black (i.e., tan) pigment.

Long Coats

The correct Shepherd coat is relatively short, with an

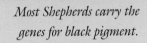

Most Shepherds carry the genes for black pigment.

The long coat is not as waterproof as the standard short coat.

obvious undercoat. As such, it is quite waterproof. Some dogs are born with long coats that usually, though not always, are devoid of undercoat.

Such coats are less useful and more difficult to groom, but many pet owners seem to like the long-coated version. Therefore, there is not strong selection against it, though very few breeders would deliberately breed from long-coated stock.

The normal coat is dominant to the long version, so we have three kinds of dog: normal, normal but carrying the long-coat gene, and long.

About 10 percent of pups are born long-coated.

OSTEOCHONDRITIS DISSECANS (OCD)

This disease is one in which there is a faulty conversion of cartilage to bone. The condition can occur in the shoulder, elbow, stifle, and hock, and treatment is less effective as you go down this list. Usually, OCD is seen at around 4 months of age, with pups that are intermittently lame. There is evidence that it is an inherited trait, with about 25 percent to 35 percent heritability. However, excess use of calcium and rapid growth are contributory factors.

PANCREATIC INSUFFICIENCY

The pancreatic gland is in the abdomen and secretes enzymes used in the digestion of food, particularly fat. The pancreas is also involved in insulin production. Exocrine pancreatic insufficiency is a condition in which pancreatic damage causes a deficiency of digestive enzymes.

Pancreatic insufficiency causes an inability to digest food.

As a result, food is not properly digested. Affected dogs lose weight while eating large quantities of food. They produce voluminous, clay-colored, foul-smelling excreta, in which much indigested food is seen. With specific medication to aid digestion, many such dogs can lead relatively normal lives. Most dogs develop the problem before they are 4 years of age.

Patent Ductus Arteriosus (PDA)

This occurs when the ductus arteriosus, which is a fetal heart feature, does not close after birth. If it partially closes, it is termed ductus diverticulum and, if it stays open, it is called PDA. As a consequence of PDA, blood is not circulated in the normal way.

The condition is controlled by many genes, and affected stock should not be bred from. The risk of PDA is not high in the breed, but are increased if dogs that are closely related to PDA cases are used for breeding.

PANOSTEITIS

This is excessive bone production on the long bones, often called bone inflammation. Seen between 5 to 12 months of age, it is an inherited trait of a polygenic nature, but with a low heritability (12 percent). It is usually something that dogs grow out of in their teenage months, though it is a painful condition during puppyhood. It is more common in the United States than elsewhere.

RIGHT AORTIC ARCH

The fourth, right aortic arch is normally only seen in the fetus, but can persist after birth. This condition, though uncommon, is more likely to be seen in the Shepherd than in any other breed. The problem results in constriction of the esophagus, which results in vomiting, difficulty in swallowing and often pneumonia.

PERIPHERAL VESTIBULAR DISEASE

A congenital defect seen in the Shepherd, it is concerned with middle ear problems. Pups develop a head tilt and circle in an unbalanced way, holding their head back or to one side. Rarely do dogs totally recover. As adults, dogs afflicted with this condition will still show some degree of head tilt in many instances. It is thought to be inherited, possibly as a simple autosomal recessive.

Dogs with middle ear problems may develop a head tilt.

Unrelated conditions affecting the esophagus (achalasia and megaesophagus) also lead to vomiting in puppies, and it is important to seek veterinary advice to ensure which problem has to be treated. Again, affected dogs ought not to be bred from.

If you are concerned about your dog's health, do not delay in seeking veterinary advice.

PITUITARY DWARFISM

Dwarf Shepherds have been known for the best part of 50 years. At birth, they are similar in size to normal puppies but, by 8 weeks of age, they are very much smaller than normal siblings. They also have shorter muzzles, and are readily distinguished from under-sized, but non-dwarf, siblings. Dwarf Shepherds eventually reach a size akin to a terrier—12 inches (30 cm)—and then grow no taller. At about 12 months of age, the puppy coat is lost and no other grown, so that the dog is hairless apart from tufts around the ears and pasterns.

SOFT EARS

All Shepherd pups are born with hanging ears, which should start to erect in the second or third month of life. During teething, carriage is not ideal, but the majority of dogs develop the correct ear carriage typical of the breed. Some have very weak musculature, so that the ears are not as firm as breeders might hope. However, some never get ear erection and remain with hanging (soft) ears. This is another simple recessive trait, in which soft ears to soft ears would give 100 percent soft ears. Most breeders reject soft-eared dogs from their breeding programs.

Von Willebrand's Disease (VWD)

This is a blood disease affecting Factor VIII, leading to symptoms that include mucosal bleeding. Inherited as a dominant condition from the gene VWD, with VWD/VWD being lethal, VWD/vwd being affected in varying degrees, and vwd/vwd being normal. Clinical severity declines with age. The disease requires blood testing by skilled laboratories to distinguish it from other defects.

It is believed to be quite common in the United States, where a prevalence of 20 percent has been suggested. In the United States, programs exist to test Shepherds for this condition. Unlike Hemophilia A, which also affects Factor VIII, VWD is seen in both sexes, as it is autosomal and not sex-linked.

A working dog at heart, the Shepherd is usually robust and healthy.

ABOUT THE AUTHOR

Dr. Malcolm Willis bought his first German Shepherd in 1953 and has owned them ever since. He first judged in 1959, gave Challenge Certificates in 1978, and has judged in nine countries around the world. For some 13 years, he was on the Council of the German Shepherd Dog League, and he has been Chairman of the German Shepherd Dog Breed Council in Britain since it was formed in the mid 1980s.

He is one of ten breed surveyors for the Breed Council (U.K.), and he runs the genetic side of the hip dysplasia scoring scheme for all breeds.

In 1988, he was awarded a gold medal by the German Shepherd Dog Council of Australia for services to the breed and, in that same year, he judged the German Shepherd Dog National in Britain, the only Briton yet to do so.